It's Easy To Play Whitney Houston.

Didn't We Almost Have It All, 6
How Will I Know, 3
I Will Always Love You, 10
I'm Every Woman, 14
My Love Is Your Love, 19
One Moment In Time, 24
Run To You, 28
So Emotional, 46
Step By Step, 32
Where Do Broken Hearts Go, 38
You Give Good Love, 42

Wise Publications
London / New York / Paris / Sydney / Copenhagen / Madrid / Tokyo

Exclusive Distributors:

Music Sales Limited
8/9 Frith Street, London W1V 5TZ, England.

Music Sales Pty Limited
120 Rothschild Avenue, Rosebery, NSW 2018, Australia.

Order No. AM941480
ISBN 0-7119-6184-0
This book © Copyright 2000 by Wise Publications.

Unauthorised reproduction of any part of this publication by any
means including photocopying is an infringement of copyright.

Cover photograph courtesy of London Features International.
Compiled by Nick Crispin.
Music arranged by Stephen Duro.
Music processed by Allegro Reproductions.

Music Sales' complete catalogue describes thousands of titles and
is available in full colour sections by subject, direct from Music Sales Limited.
Please state your areas of interest and send a cheque/postal order for £1.50 for postage to:
Music Sales Limited, Newmarket Road, Bury St. Edmunds, Suffolk IP33 3YB.

www.musicsales.com

Your Guarantee of Quality:
As publishers, we strive to produce every book to the highest commercial standards.
The music has been freshly engraved and the book has been carefully designed to minimise awkward page turns and to make playing from it a real pleasure.
Particular care has been given to specifying acid-free, neutral-sized paper made from pulps which have not been elemental chlorine bleached.
This pulp is from farmed sustainable forests and was produced with special regard for the environment.
Throughout, the printing and binding have been planned to ensure a sturdy, attractive publication which should give years of enjoyment.
If your copy fails to meet our high standards, please inform us and we will gladly replace it.

Printed in the United Kingdom by
Caligraving Limited, Thetford, Norfolk.

This publication is not authorised for sale in
the United States of America and/or Canada.

How Will I Know

Words & Music by George Merrill, Shannon Rubicam & Narada Michael Walden

Verse 3:

Oh, wake me, I'm shakin'; wish I had you near me now.
Said there's no mistakin'; what I feel is really love.
How will I know? (Girl, trust your feelings.)
How will I know?
How will I know? (Love can be deceiving.)
How will I know?

Didn't We Almost Have It All

Words & Music by Michael Masser & Will Jennings

© Copyright 1982 Prince Street Music & Blue Sky Rider Songs/Irving Music Incorporated, USA.
Rights administered on behalf of Prince Street Music by
Chelsea Music Publishing Company Limited, 124 Great Portland Street, London W1(50%).
Rights administered on behalf of Blue Sky Rider Songs/Irving Music Incorporated by
Rondor Music (London) Limited, 10a Parsons Green, London SW6 (50%).
All Rights Reserved. International Copyright Secured.

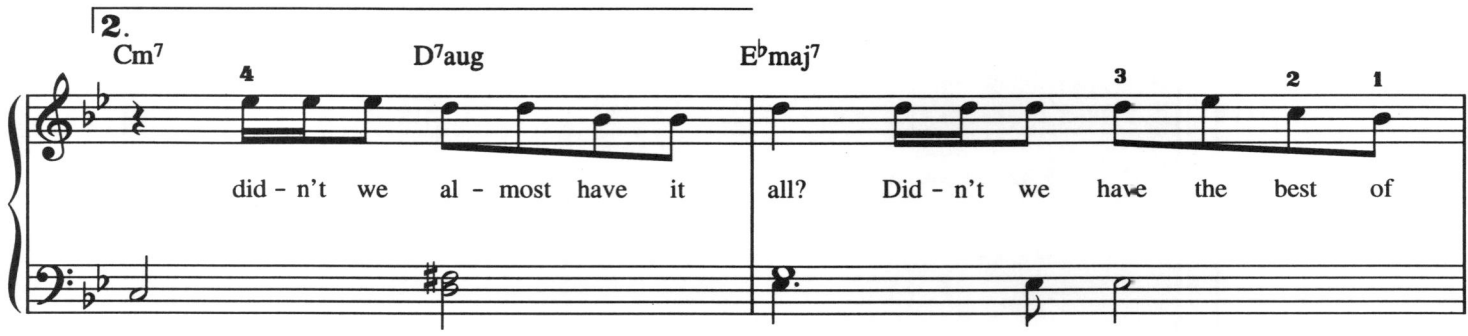
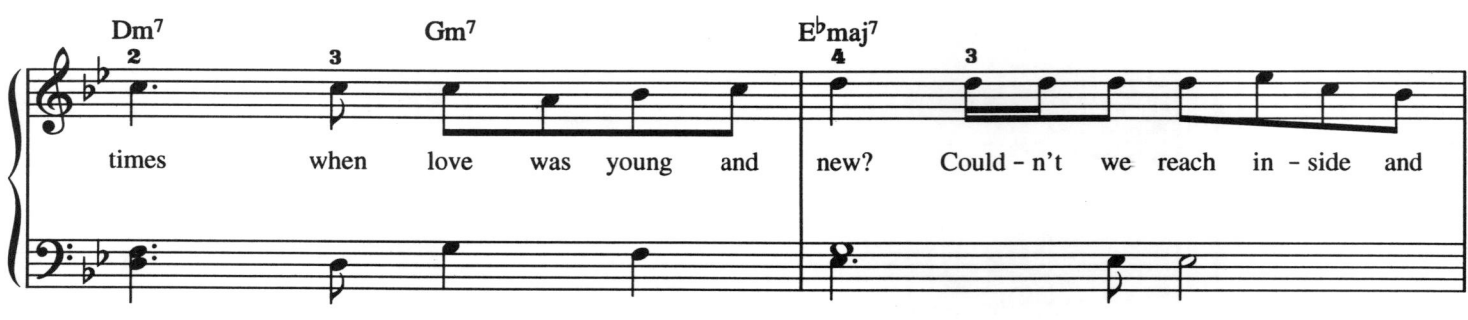

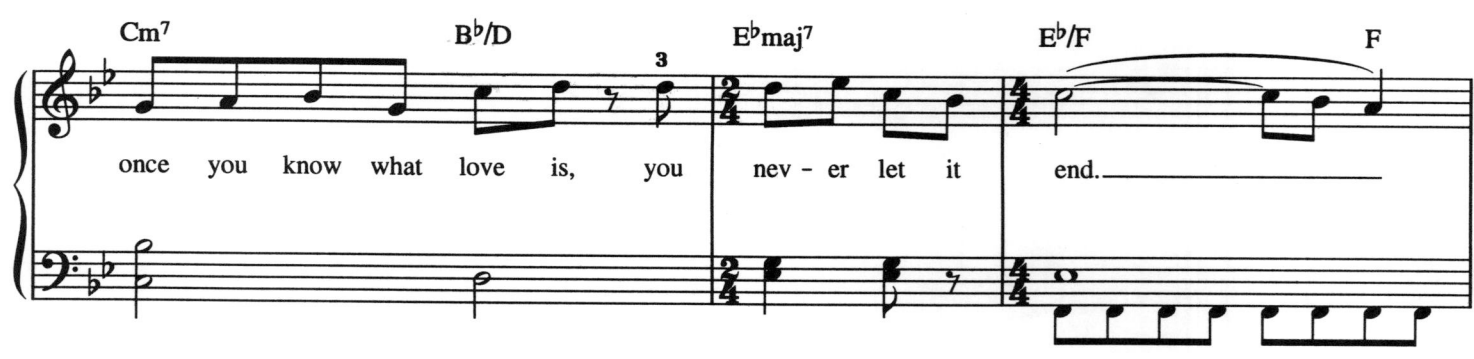

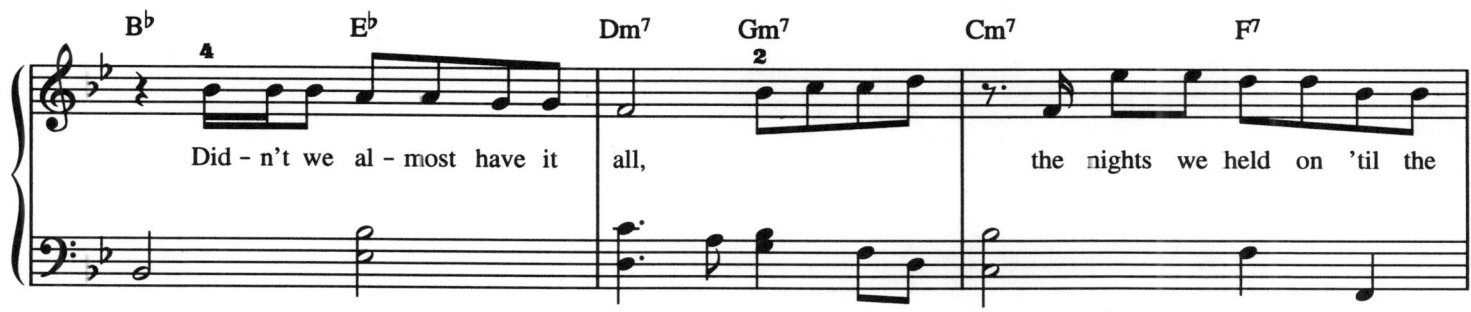
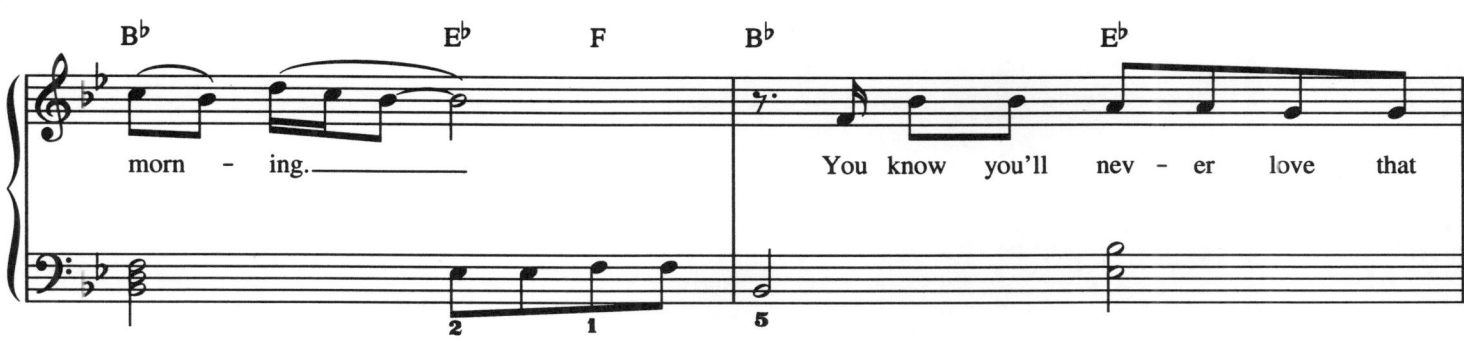
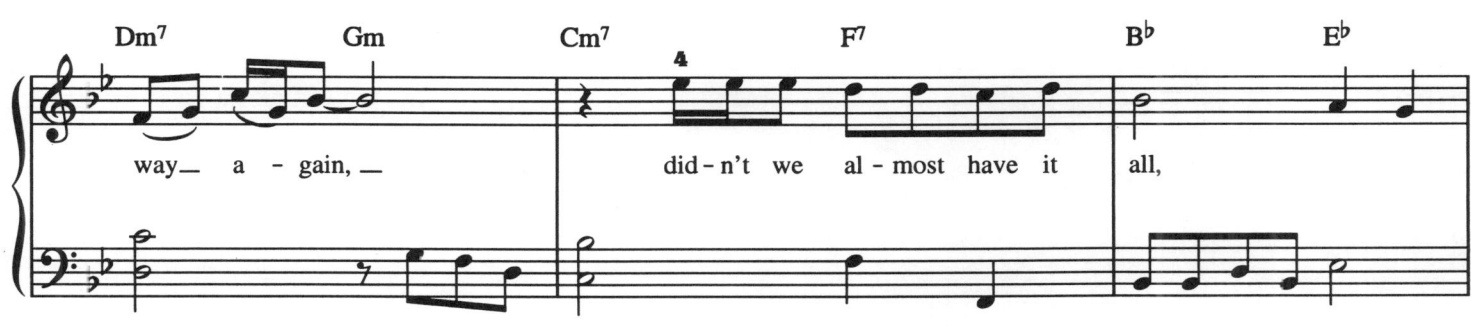
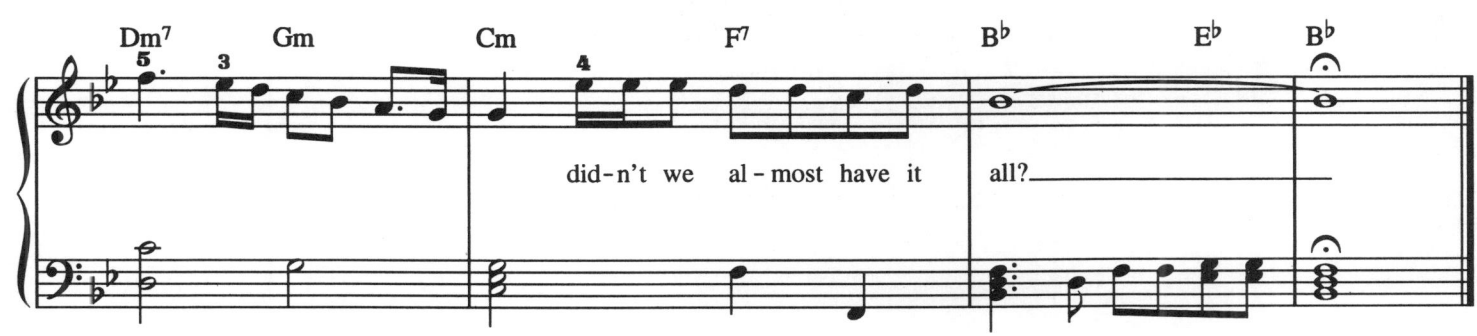

I Will Always Love You

Words & Music by Dolly Parton

© Copyright 1975 Velvet Apple Music, USA.
Carlin Music Corporation, Iron Bridge House, 3 Bridge Approach, London NW1.
All Rights Reserved. International Copyright Secured.

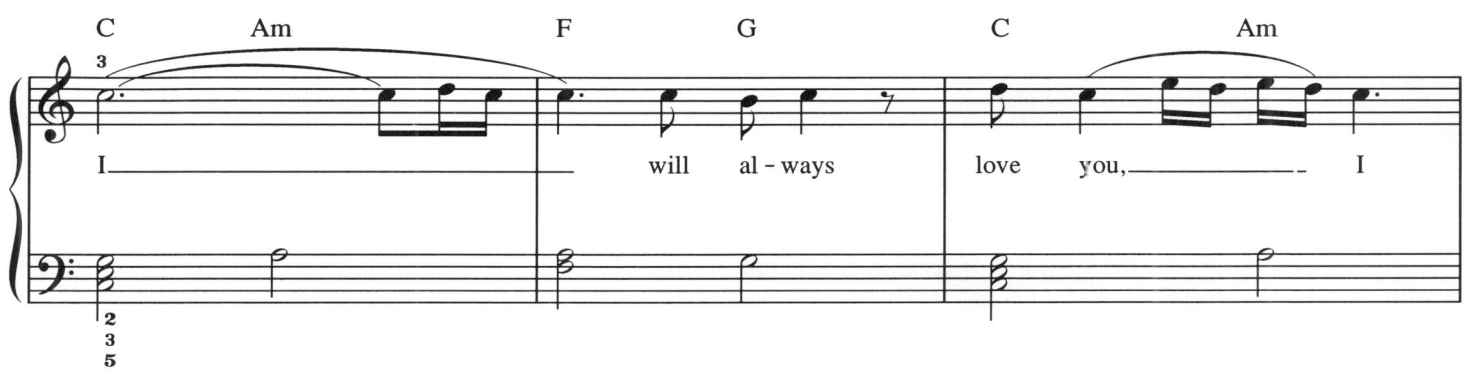

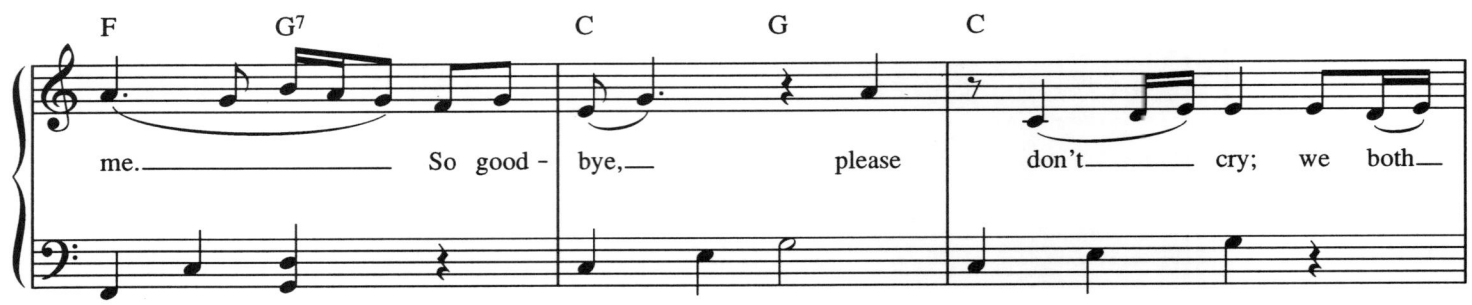
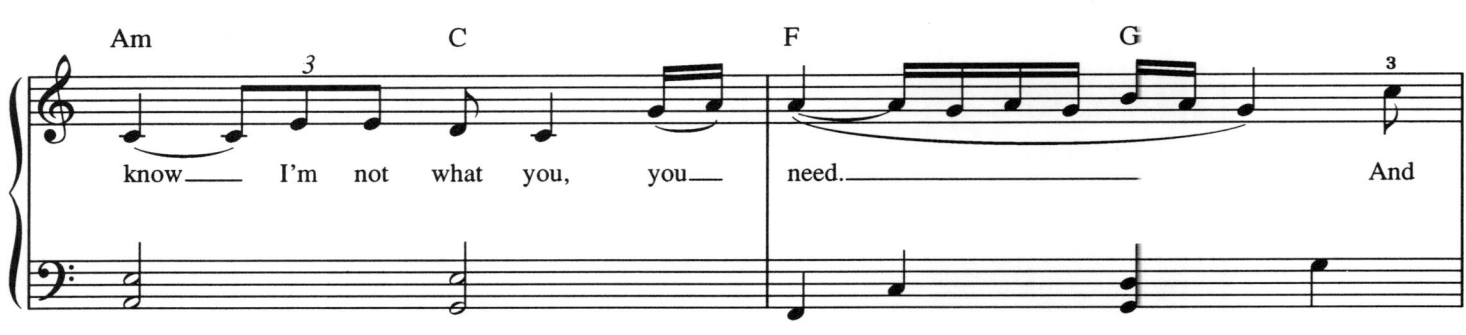
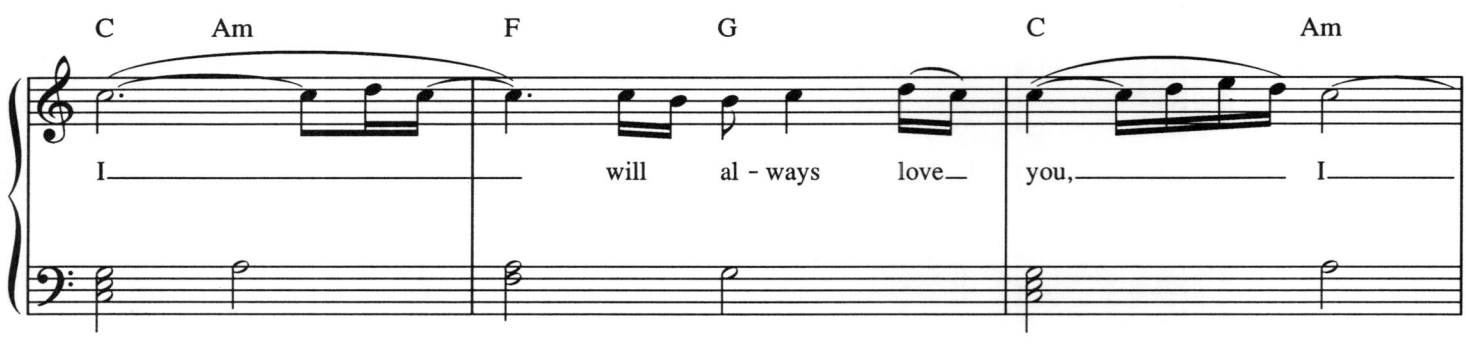
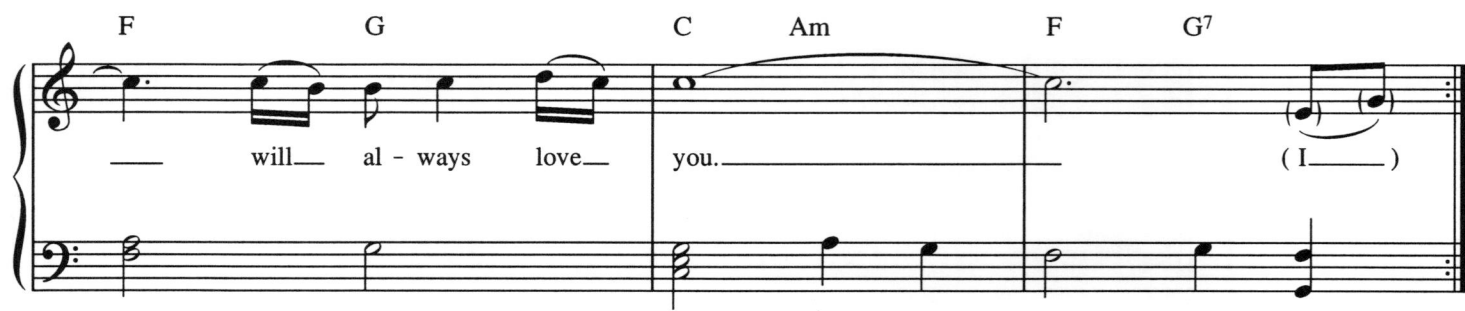

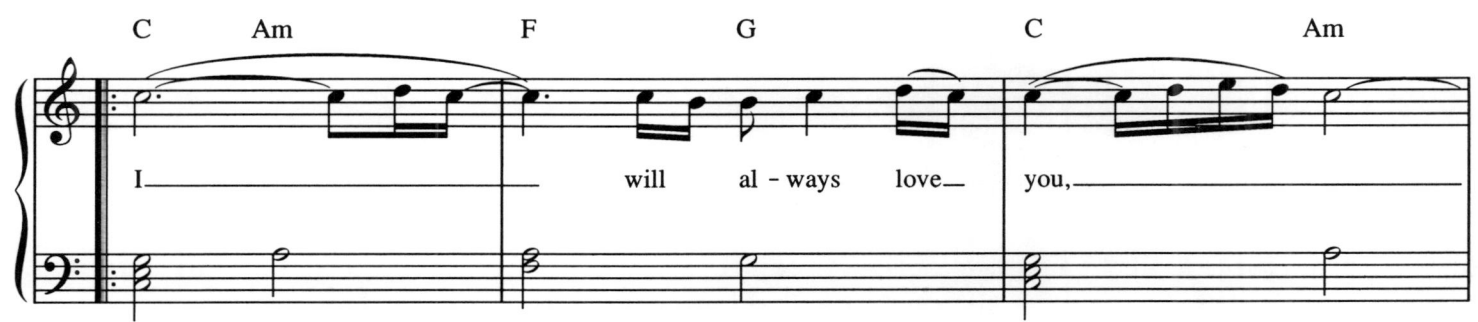
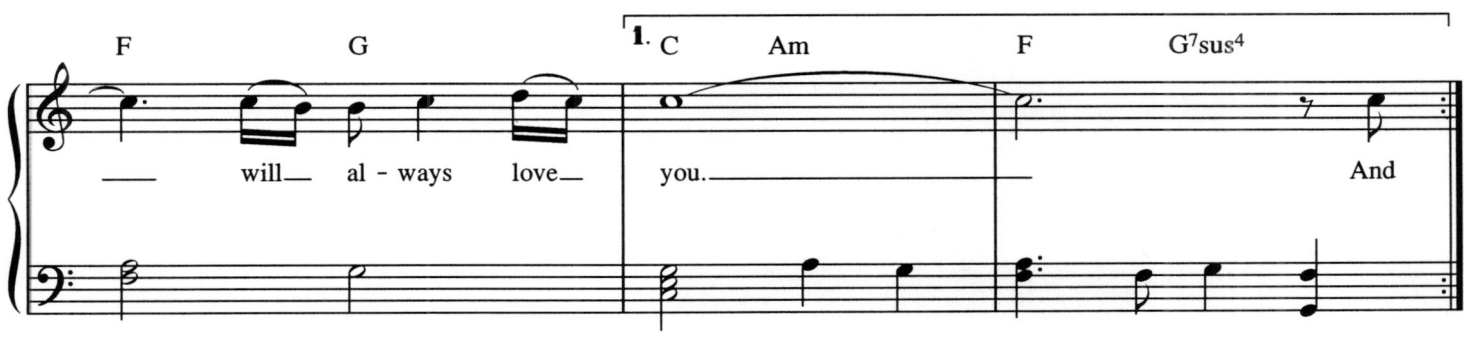
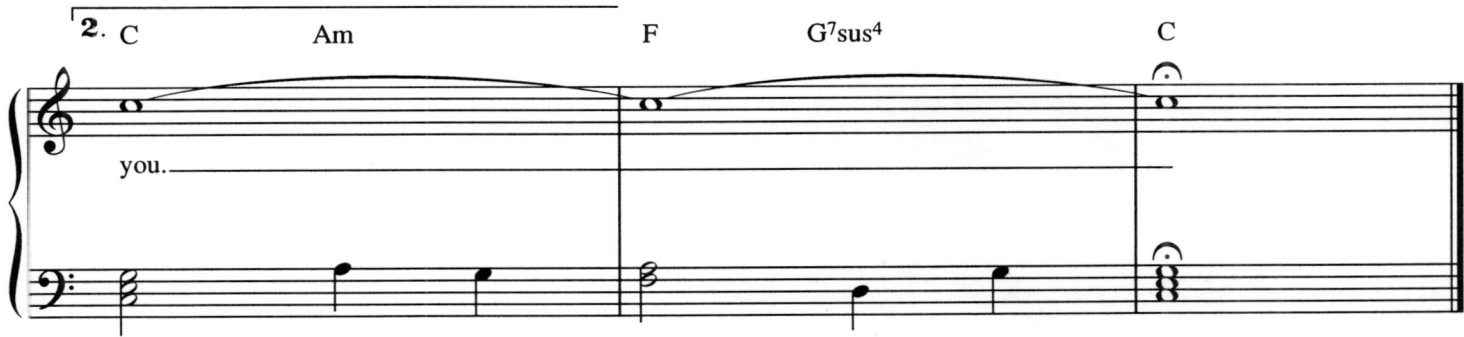

Verse 2:

I hope life treats you kind,
And I hope you have all that you ever dreamed of,
And I wish you joy and happiness,
But above all this, I wish you love.

I'm Every Woman

Words & Music by Nickolas Ashford & Valerie Simpson

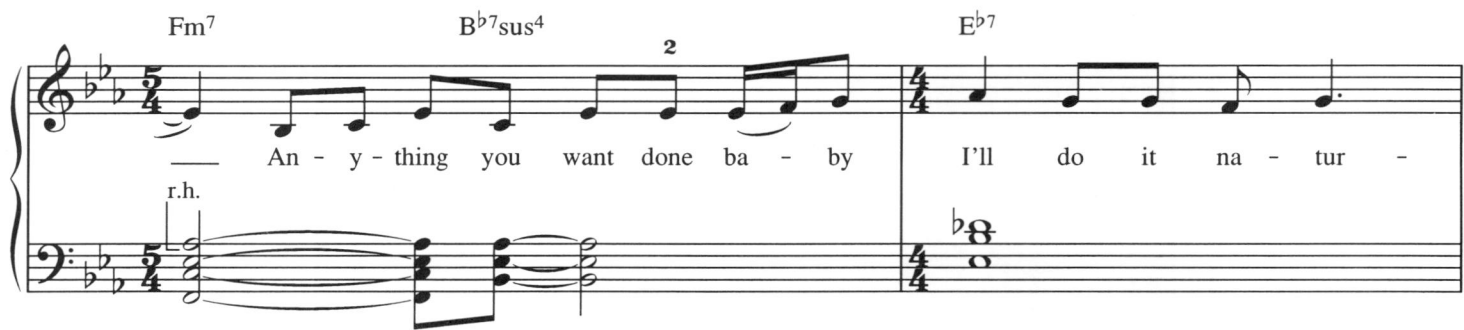

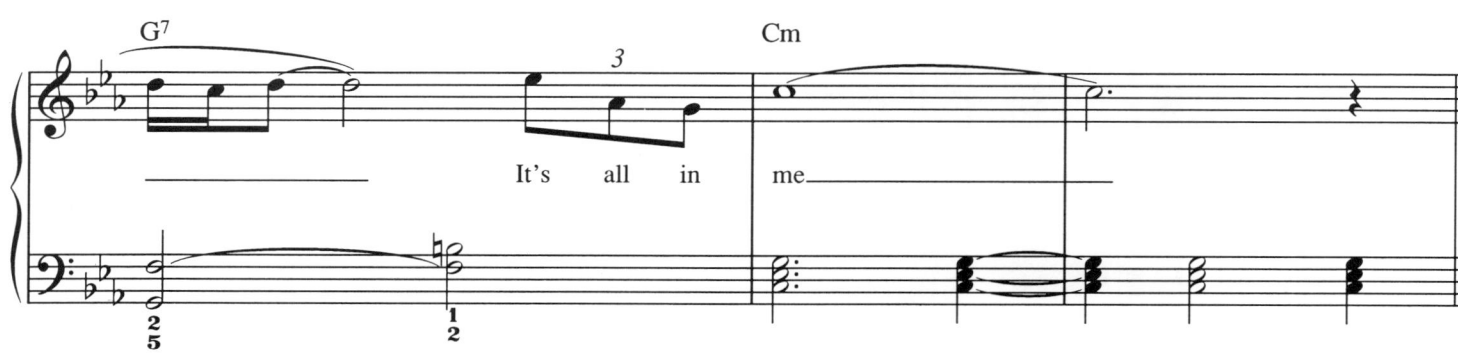

My Love Is Your Love

Words & Music by Wyclef Jean & Jerry Duplessis

Moderately slow with a beat

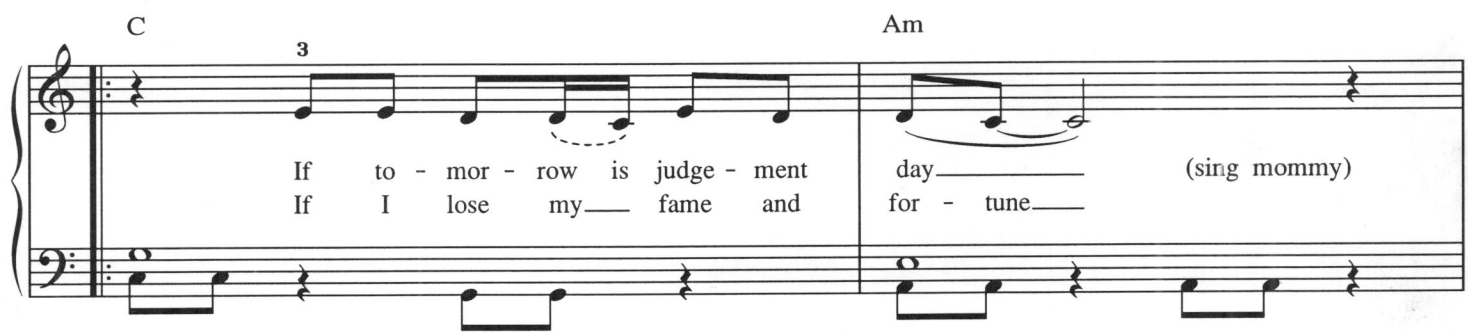

© Copyright 1998 Sony/ATV Tunes LLC/Huss Zwingli Publishing Incorporated &
TeBass Music/EMI-Blackwood Music Incorporated, USA.
Sony/ATV Music Publishing (UK) Limited, 10 Great Marlborough Street, London W1 (75%)/
EMI Music Publishing Limited, 127 Charing Cross Road, London WC2 (25%).
All Rights Reserved. International Copyright Secured.

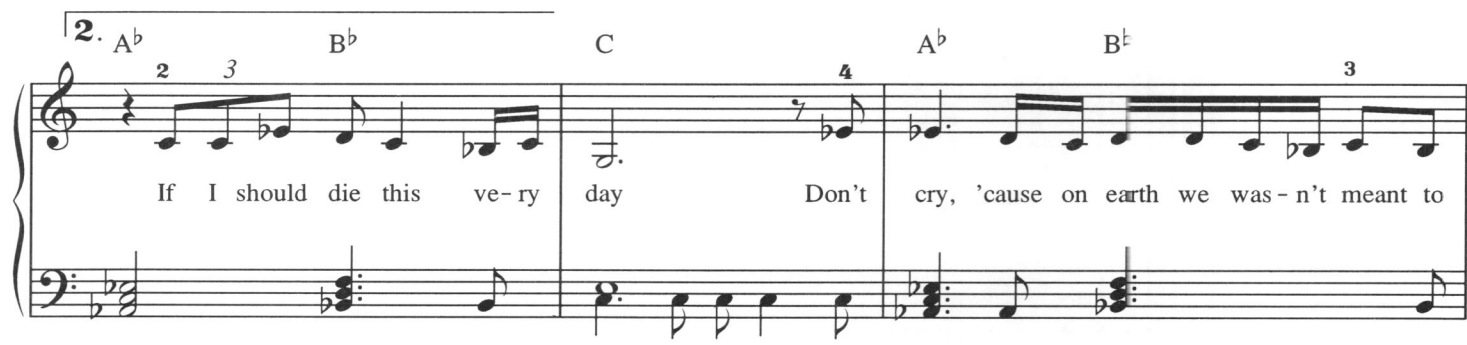
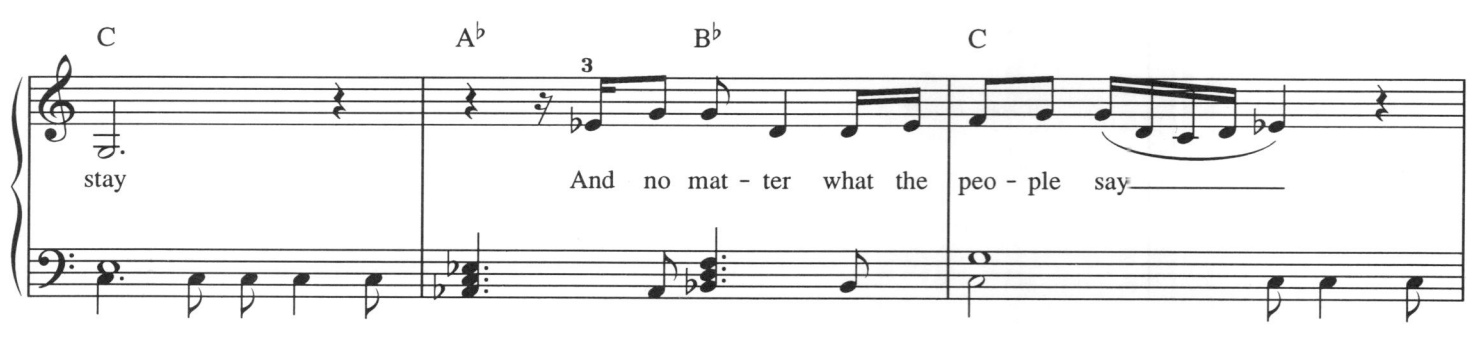

22

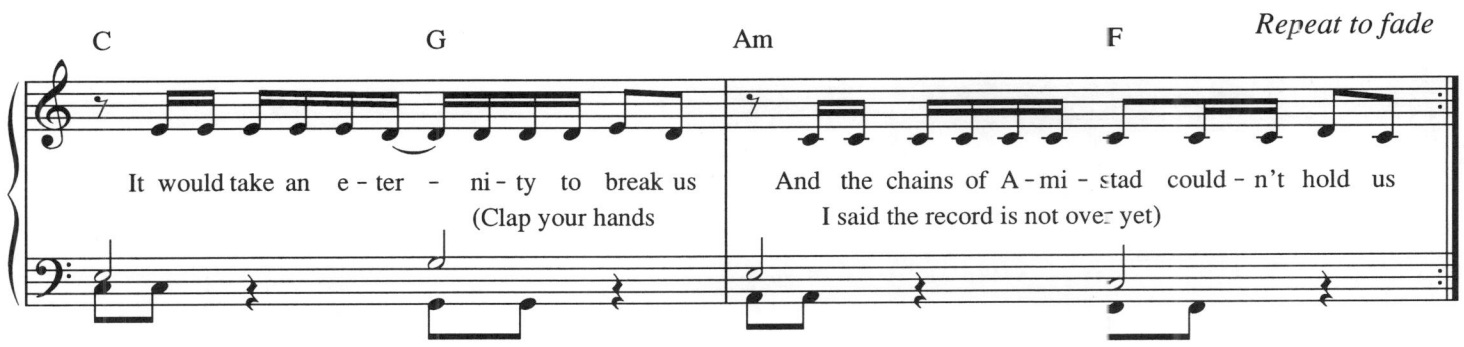

One Moment In Time

Words & Music by Albert Hammond & John Bettis

© Copyright 1988 WB Music Corporation, Albert Hammond Enterprises Incorporated & John Bettis Music, USA.
Windswept Pacific Music Limited, Hope House, 40 St. Peter's Road, London W6 (50%)/
Warner Chappell Music Limited, Griffin House, 161 Hammersmith Road, London W6 (50%).
All Rights Reserved. International Copyright Secured.

Run To You

Words & Music by Jud Friedman and Allan Rich

© Copyright 1991 MCA Music Incorporated/Nelana Songs & PSO Limited/Music By Candlelight, USA.
Peermusic (UK) Limited, 8-14 Verulam Street, London WC1 (50%) &
Universal/MCA Music Limited, 77 Fulham Palace Road, London W6 (50%).
All Rights Reserved. International Copyright Secured.

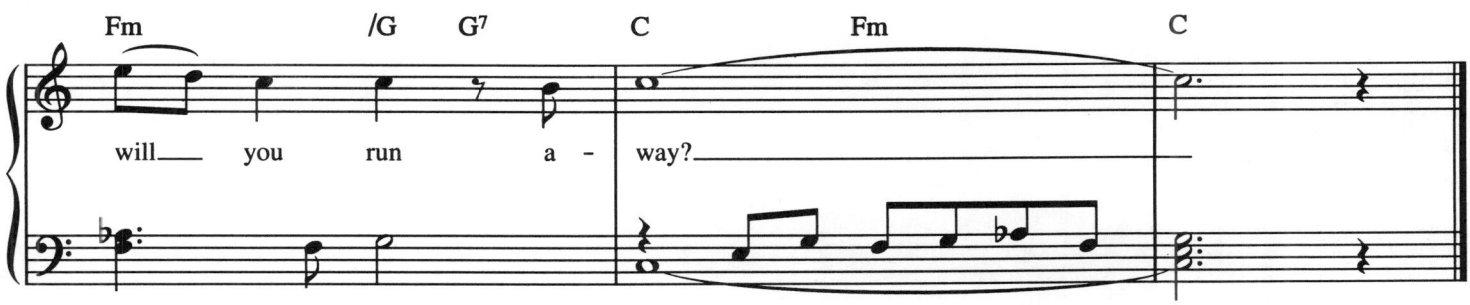

Verse 2:

Each day, each day I play the role of someone
Always in control,
But at night I come home and turn the key,
There's nobody there,
No one cares for me.
Oh, what's the sense of trying hard to find your dreams
Without someone to share them with?
Tell me, what does it mean?

Step By Step

Words & Music by Annie Lennox

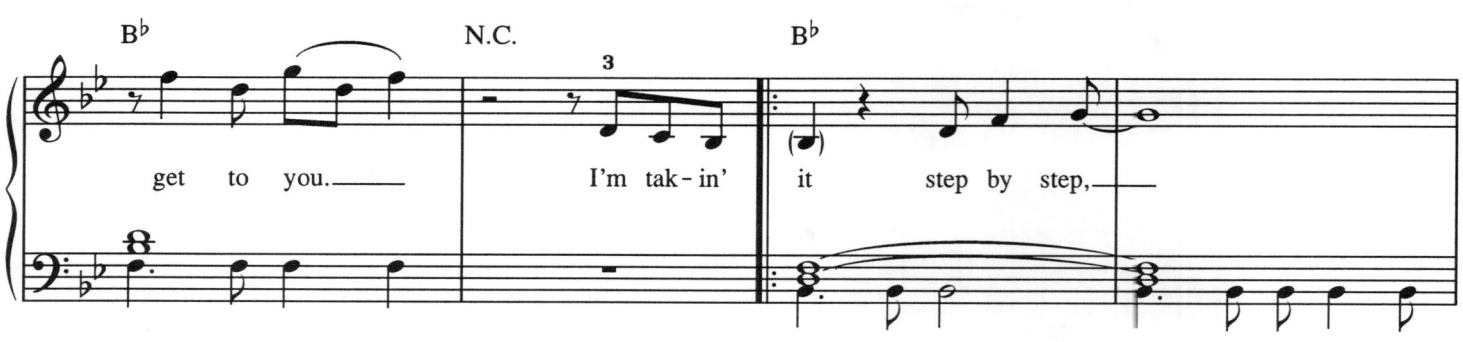

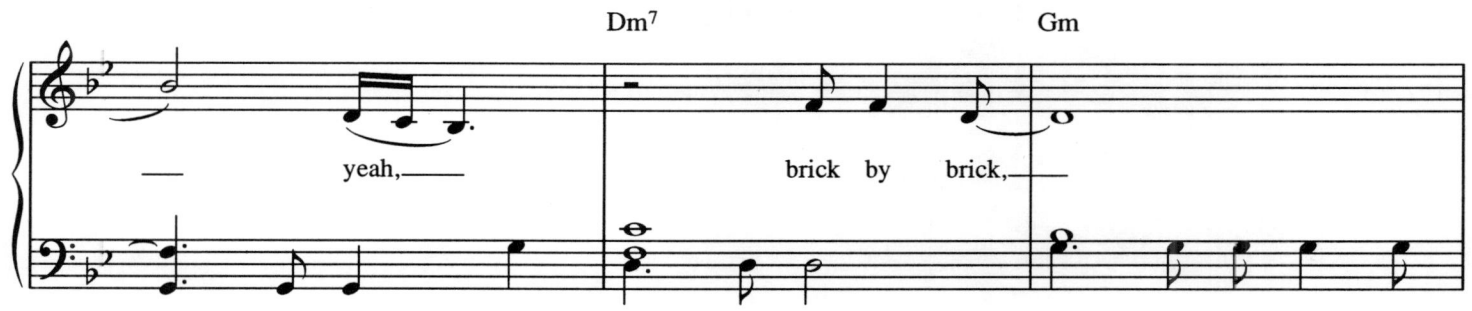

Where Do Broken Hearts Go

Words & Music by Frank Wildhorn & Chuck Jackson

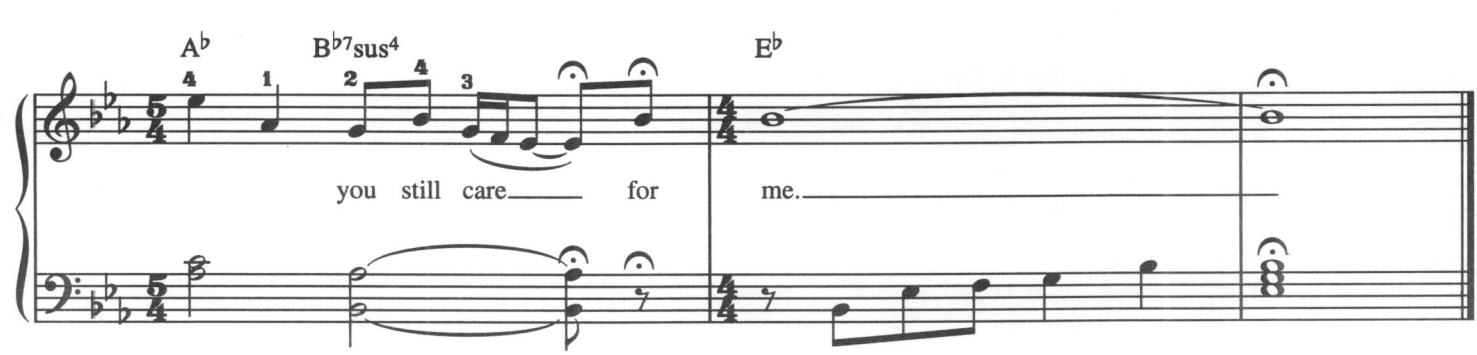

You Give Good Love

Words & Music by LaLa

So Emotional

Words & Music by Billy Steinberg & Tom Kelly

Verse 2:

I gotta watch you walk in the room, baby;
I gotta watch you walk out.
I like the animal way you move,
And when you talk I just watch your mouth.

Oh, I remember the way that we touch;
I wish I didn't like it so much.